IT HELD

Zhaoxun Yun

It Held

Copyright © 2026 by Zhaoxun Yun

All rights reserved.

No part of this book may be reproduced or transmitted in any form or by any means without prior written permission of the publisher, except for brief quotations and other non-commercial uses permitted by law.

First published as It Held (paperback) in the United States by Fovere Books, 2026.

ISBN 979-8-9949071-0-8 (paperback)

ISBN 979-8-9949071-1-5 (ebook)

Library of Congress Control Number: 2026904431

Printed in the United States of America

For permission requests or bulk purchase inquiries, contact Fovere Books at www.foverebooks.com or foverebooks@yahoo.com.

FOVERE BOOKS
Where thought finds warmth
www.foverebooks.com

First Movement

I don't remember when I first started looking at the night sky.

I mean, I know I must have done it as a kid. Everyone does. You lie on your back, the grass scratches a little, the air smells like summer or dust, and someone points up and says, that one's a star. You nod, even if you don't really know what that means yet.

But that's not the kind of looking I'm talking about.

I'm talking about the kind that comes later.

The kind that shows up after someone you love is gone.

No one tells you to do it. You don't plan it. One night, you just find yourself outside, standing there longer than you meant to, your neck starting to ache, your hands in your pockets.

The sky hasn't changed.

That's the strange part.

It looks exactly the same as it always did.

And yet you're not.

People like to talk about time.

They'll say time heals.

They'll say time moves on.

They'll say enough time has passed.

1

But when it's you, standing there in the dark, those sentences don't make it into your chest.

They're like drops of water on oiled paper. They roll around for a second, shining a little, and then—zip—they slide right off. They won't stick. No matter how carefully you try to hold them there.

I can tell you the date.

I can tell you the year.

I can even do the math, if you want.

I've done it more than once.

Sometimes I get the numbers wrong.

Not because my memory is bad, but because they don't seem to matter the way people expect them to. Twenty years. Two years. Six. When I'm standing under that sky, none of those numbers feel any closer to whatever this is than the others.

What feels real is smaller than that.

The way my chest suddenly carries a bit of weight.

The way a thought lands and doesn't leave.

The way someone who is gone can still feel close enough to reach.

Maybe they're right. I'm not here to argue. I've learned that explanations don't bring anyone back, and they don't make the nights any quieter either.

And explanation isn't always what you're asking for.

Sometimes you're just asking to be allowed to stand there and feel what you feel, without being told it's late, or misplaced, or out of order.

I don't look at the sky because I think it has answers.

I know the light is old. I know what we're seeing already happened a long time ago. I've read enough, listened enough, to understand that part.

That knowledge doesn't do much when you're actually there.

There's another thing people like to say.

They'll say, You have to let go.

Most of the time, they don't mean any harm. Usually they're trying to help. It sounds reasonable. Clean. Like one of those phrases that helps the day keep moving.

But I've always wondered what they think that actually looks like.

Let go of what, exactly?

And once it's let go, where is it supposed to land?

No one ever seems to stick around for that part.

I've noticed something else too. The people who tell you to let go usually have empty hands. When they say it, they're not carrying anything. If there's nothing pressing on your shoulders, nothing warm and familiar sitting in your palms, it's easy advice to give.

But when you've really held something—

a person,

a voice,

a way of living—

your hands don't forget that shape so quickly.

Even when they're empty, they remember.

I've tried, you know. I really have. Nothing dramatic. Just small, ordinary attempts. Keeping myself busy. Changing a few routines. Saying the right things to myself at the right times. Doing what looks sensible from the outside.

Most of it works fine during the day.

It's the unguarded moments that don't cooperate.

Early mornings.

Late nights.

Those few seconds before sleep, when you haven't shut the door inside yet.

That's when things come back. Not because you called them. But because they never actually moved out.

People tend to think holding on is an action. Like you're clenching your fists, refusing to open them. But most of the time, it doesn't feel like that at all.

It feels more like walking with a weight you've been carrying for so long you stopped noticing it.

You're moving along just fine.

Then someone points and says, That looks heavy.

And only then do you feel it.

I don't think letting go is the opposite of holding on.

I think people talk about letting go because they get uneasy watching you move through the world with certain things still with you. That doesn't mean you're weak. It doesn't mean you're stuck.

It just means those things have worked their way into how you walk.

You don't go around trying to grab your own shadow.

That kind of presence doesn't make a big show of itself.

You might not notice it right away. But later, when you look back, you realize something important happened.

You weren't hurried along.

You weren't treated like a problem to be handled.

You weren't gently pushed into a brighter mood.

You were allowed to stay where you already were.

I've learned to be a little careful with comfort. Not to refuse it outright, just not to mistake it for respect.

Sometimes what a person needs isn't to feel better. Sometimes what they need is to be understood—or at least, not corrected.

There's a difference.

Comfort wants the pain to disappear. Being properly seen is willing to stay while it doesn't.

I don't always choose right myself. Some days I want the soft words. Some days I don't have the energy to be looked at too closely.

But when I think about the moments that really stayed with me, they weren't the ones where someone tried to make things easier.

They were the ones where someone treated what I was going through as something real. Something that didn't need to be rushed past.

No fixing.

No lesson.

No hurry.

Just a quiet sense that this—whatever it was—mattered enough to sit with.

There's a moment people don't talk about much.

It's the moment when being understood quietly turns into being hurried.

At first, it feels like a relief. Someone listens. Someone nods. Someone says, I get it. And for a while, that really is enough. It's good to know your words don't just fall on the floor.

But then the pace picks up.

Not all at once. Nothing obvious. Just little nudges. Like a guide clearing their throat.

We've spent some time here.

There's more ahead.

You don't want to miss the next stop.

They're still kind. Still well-meaning. And that's what makes it hard to argue with.

Because now there's a schedule.

Now there's this sense that whatever you're feeling ought to be wrapping up. That it's been… adequate. Long enough. Healthy enough.

I've felt that before. That quiet embarrassment, like I've stayed too long in a place I was only supposed to pass through. Like I should be packing up my feelings already.

Funny thing is, I'm old enough that I should know better.

And yet there I am, feeling sheepish about still being sad. As if that's something I ought to apologize for.

I see it from the other side too.

When someone else is hurting, I catch myself doing the same thing. Glancing down at some invisible ruler. Wondering how long this usually takes. Whether what they're carrying has gone past the "normal" mark.

That's not cruelty.

That's fear.

We're scared of places with no clear exit. We're scared of standing still too long, because we don't know what it says about us.

So we turn understanding into encouragement.

Encouragement into guidance.

And before we notice, guidance turns into a kind of watching.

Not harsh. Just… attentive. Waiting.

That's when I start to pull back. When I feel eyes on me, checking if I'm done yet. Checking if I'm ready to move on.

It's like being on a walking tour.

Everyone's heading for the next landmark. And I'm the one who wants to stop for a minute. There's a bare tree by the road. A puddle reflecting the sky. Nothing special, really—but something about it asks to be looked at.

The guide keeps waving ahead.

And me? I'm not stuck.

I'm just… slower.

Some views don't open up at full speed.

So I've learned to let people walk on.

Not in anger.

Not in bitterness.

More like with a tired smile.

I know they mean well. I know they're trying to help me get somewhere better.

I just don't think better is always ahead.

Sometimes it's right where you're standing.

And staying there doesn't take courage so much as patience. The kind that lets you sit until your legs go a little numb. Until the light shifts. Until the shadow at your feet moves on its own.

That's usually when I know I've stayed long enough.

Not because someone told me it was time.

But because the world did.

After a while, even standing still starts to feel like something you're doing wrong.

Not loudly wrong. No one points it out. No one stops you. It's quieter than that. More like the faint pressure you feel when you realize everyone else has already moved on to the next thing, and you're still where you were.

Nothing dramatic happens.

The street doesn't change.

The sky doesn't answer.

The night doesn't close in or open up.

It just keeps being what it is.

And somehow, that constancy becomes harder to bear than noise would have been.

I've noticed that stillness only looks peaceful from a distance. Up close, it has edges. You feel them when you stay too long. Your legs start to complain. Your thoughts circle back on themselves. The same memory passes through again, slightly dulled, slightly heavier, like a coin that's been handled too many times.

People think staying means resting.

It doesn't always.

Sometimes staying is work. Not the kind you can point to, or explain afterward. Just the quiet effort of not pushing yourself forward for the sake of looking functional.

I didn't set out to learn this. I would have preferred something clearer. A rule, maybe. Or at least a sign that says: you can stop here, and no one will mark it against you.

But there aren't signs like that.

There's only the slow realization that nothing is going to step in and release you. No bell rings. No voice announces that the required time has been served.

You just remain.

At first, that feels like a choice.

Later, it doesn't.

It feels more like a condition you've entered without noticing the door close behind you.

I used to think conditions were things you could identify cleanly. Illness. Weather. Debt. Situations with names. Situations other people recognized.

This doesn't come with a name.

It doesn't even come with clear symptoms. You function. You speak. You show up. You answer when spoken to. From the outside, nothing seems out of place.

And yet something is no longer adjustable.

You can't rush it.

You can't bargain with it.

You can't improve it by being reasonable.

You find yourself moving more carefully, not because you're afraid, but because pushing doesn't produce anything new. The effort goes out, but nothing comes back.

That's usually when impatience sets in.

Not other people's impatience—your own.

You start watching yourself. Timing your reactions. Asking whether this is still necessary. Whether you're lingering out of habit, or stubbornness, or something less flattering.

Those questions don't help much either.

They just add another layer of noise.

There's a particular kind of exhaustion that comes from trying to justify your own pace. From rehearsing explanations no one explicitly asked for. From carrying a quiet sense that you owe the world a cleaner version of yourself than the one you currently have.

I've felt that weight more than once.

It settles somewhere between the shoulders. Not sharp. Not painful. Just persistent. Like a hand that never quite lifts away.

The strange thing is, the world doesn't actually demand any of this.

It goes on whether you hurry or not.

Cars pass. Lights change. People laugh somewhere you can't see. The machinery of ordinary life keeps running, indifferent to whether you've sorted yourself out.

That indifference can feel cruel.

But sometimes it's also a kind of relief.

It means you're not holding anything up.

You're not delaying history.

You're not failing a test.

You're not blocking the way forward for anyone else.

You're simply… not moving yet.

I've learned that there's a limit to how much meaning you can extract from this state.

At a certain point, interpretation starts to feel forced. You notice yourself reaching for lessons, metaphors, conclusions—anything that might turn this stretch of time into something useful.

That urge fades eventually.

Not because it's satisfied, but because it runs out of energy.

What remains after that isn't insight. It's quieter. Less impressive.

It's the fact of being there.

Breathing.

Waiting.

Letting the hours arrange themselves without your help.

This isn't peace. I wouldn't call it that.

Peace implies arrival. Or at least agreement.

This feels more provisional. Like you're camped out somewhere you didn't intend to stay, but haven't found a reason to leave.

You keep an eye on the horizon, not expecting anything in particular—just out of habit. You notice small changes. The way the air cools. The way sounds thin out. The way your body adjusts to standing this way.

Eventually, the strain eases a little.

Not because anything resolved, but because your muscles learned how to hold themselves here.

That adjustment matters.

It's subtle enough that you might miss it if you weren't paying attention. But once it happens, you know you've crossed into a different phase. Not better. Not worse. Just different.

You're no longer actively trying to get somewhere else.

You're here.

That's when people usually expect a turn. A shift in tone. A sign that something has been gained.

There isn't one.

If anything, the gain is that the pressure to gain something has loosened.

You stop asking what this is for.

You stop wondering how it will look later.

You stop measuring it against some imagined future where everything lines up neatly.

What's left isn't an answer.

It's a kind of tolerance.

For the unfinished. For the unredeemed. For the parts of life that don't present themselves as steps in a larger story.

I don't think this state changes people in any essential way.

It doesn't promise improvement.

What it does, sometimes, is remove the expectation that anything should.

And that absence—of expectation, of direction, of urgency—creates a space that isn't comfortable, but is workable.

You can stand in it without pretending. Without preparing an explanation. Without bracing for what comes next.

You're not done.

But you're not required to be.

For now, that's enough.

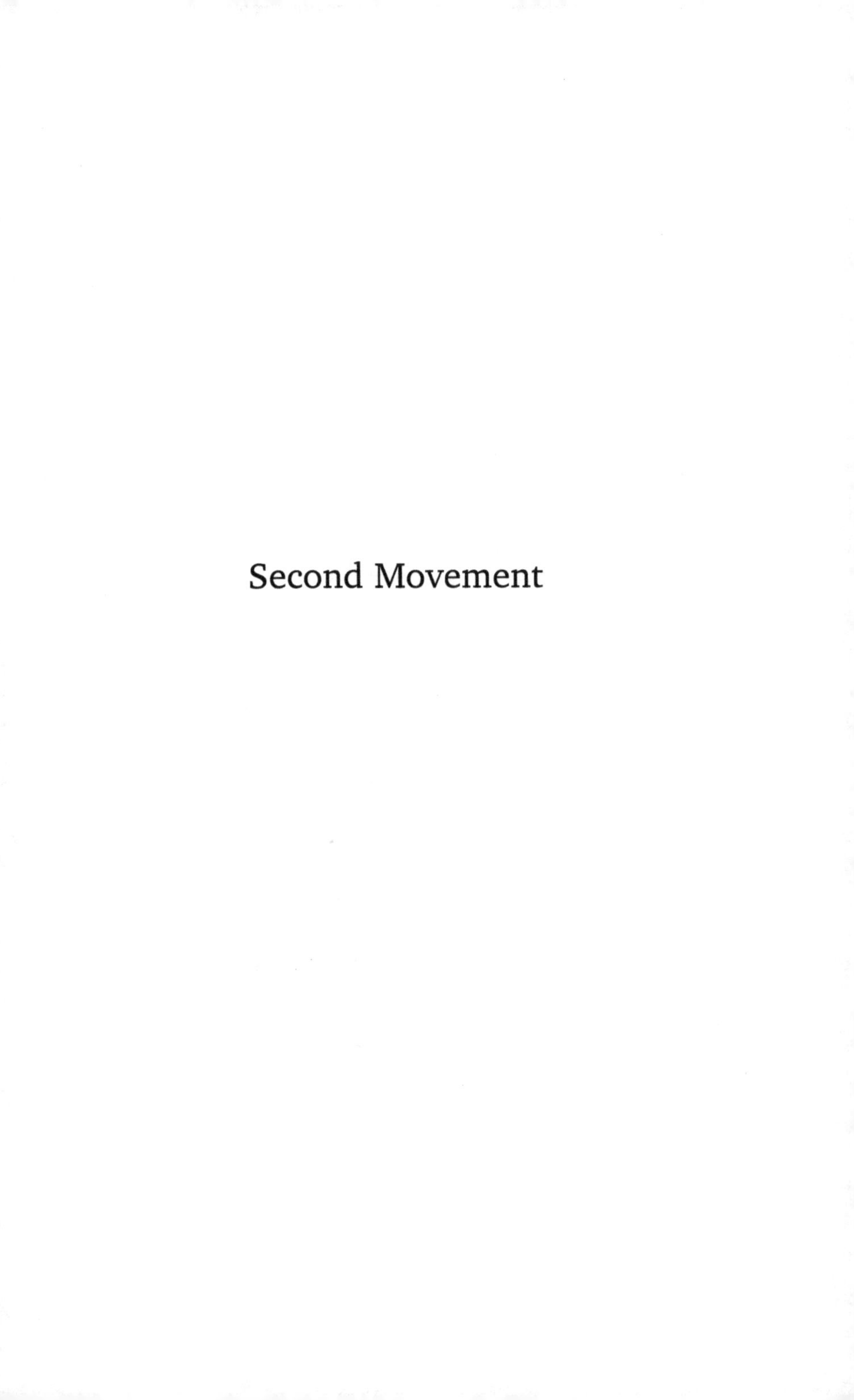

Second Movement

The flower was already there when I noticed it.

That's important, I think.

Not something I arrived with. Not something arranged for effect. Just something I nearly missed.

It was growing out of a narrow crack along the side of the building, where the concrete had split just enough to let a thin line of dirt collect. A place no one would have chosen on purpose. Too close to the wall. Too dry. Too exposed.

I stopped without deciding to.

It wasn't a conscious pause. More like my body slowed before my thoughts caught up. One step shorter than the last. My foot landing flat instead of rolling forward.

The flower wasn't doing particularly well.

One petal had curled in on itself. Another was torn, as if something had brushed past too hard and not noticed. The stem leaned at an awkward angle, bending toward the street, where there was more light but also more traffic.

I don't know what kind it was.

That used to bother me. I used to feel a small itch when I couldn't name things. As if knowing the category would somehow stabilize what I was looking at.

Now it mostly just feels unnecessary.

The flower didn't seem to care whether I recognized it.

I stood there longer than I meant to. Not long enough to draw attention, but long enough to feel slightly out of sync with the rhythm of the sidewalk. People passed behind me. A bike cut through the narrow space between curb and wall. Someone brushed my sleeve and kept going.

No one looked down.

That wasn't surprising. There was nothing down there that demanded to be seen.

I crouched, then straightened again. The movement felt stiff, like my knees had forgotten how often I used to do this. I adjusted my weight, trying to find a position that didn't strain anything.

Up close, the flower looked worse.

The edges of the petals were dry. The color had faded unevenly, brighter near the center, dull toward the tips. There was no symmetry left to admire. No clean shape.

It wasn't dying in any dramatic way.
It just wasn't thriving.

I caught myself thinking: *Someone should move it.*

The thought arrived fully formed, before I could stop it. A small, practical idea. If it were somewhere else—somewhere softer, somewhere with more space—it might have a chance.

Then I realized how absurd that was.

I didn't know where it had come from. I didn't know how deep its roots went. I didn't know whether moving it would help or finish it off.

The idea dissolved almost as soon as it appeared.

I've noticed that this happens a lot. The impulse to intervene shows up first, confident and quick. The reasons it won't work follow more slowly, like someone arriving late to a conversation that's already winding down.

I stayed anyway.

Not because staying would improve anything, but because leaving felt dishonest. Like turning away just to preserve a sense of usefulness.

A car passed close enough that I felt the air shift against my calf. The flower trembled, barely. Not enough to break. Just enough to register the disturbance.

That was all.

No response beyond that. No adjustment. No sign that my presence, or the passing car, or the patch of light had changed anything essential.

For a moment, I waited for something more.

A thought.

A feeling.

A lesson.

Nothing came.

The absence wasn't dramatic. It didn't announce itself. It just sat there, the way silence does after a sound you thought would echo longer.

I became aware of how long I'd been there. Of the dull pressure in my heels. Of the fact that my back had begun to tighten slightly, the way it does when I lean forward too long.

This wasn't a meaningful moment. At least, it didn't feel like one.

It was just a moment that hadn't turned into anything else.

That used to bother me too—I used to think moments were supposed to add up.

That if you paid attention carefully enough, you could gather them into something coherent. Something you could carry away.

Standing there, I realized how thin that expectation had become.

The flower didn't offer itself as an example.

It didn't stand in for anything.

It didn't ask to be understood.

It existed, narrowly, under conditions it hadn't chosen.

I straightened up slowly. My legs protested, briefly, then settled. I looked once more, not to memorize it, just to acknowledge that it had been there.

There was no sense of completion.

No quiet satisfaction.

No feeling of having done the right thing.

I hadn't helped.

I hadn't harmed.

I hadn't learned anything that could be applied elsewhere.

I stepped back into the flow of the sidewalk.

The rhythm picked up around me immediately. Shoes striking pavement. Voices overlapping. The ordinary forward pull of the street reclaiming its pace.

After a few steps, I tried to recall the exact color of the petals.

I couldn't.

That felt honest.

It remained what it was: something seen, briefly, without being absorbed into a larger story.

And then it was left behind.

THIRD MOVEMENT

The glass door stuck for half a second before it opened.
Not broken. Just swollen in its frame, like it had learned the weather too well.

A bell rang. Too bright for the hour. Too eager.

Inside, the air was sharp with cold and sugar. Refrigerators lined the wall, humming in different keys, each one slightly out of tune with the next. Fluorescent lights flattened everything they touched—faces, labels, the color of hands. Nothing hid in here. Everything was meant to be seen.

I stood just inside the door longer than I needed to. Let the warmth fall off me. Let the floor stop rocking.

A man in a baseball cap was arguing with the lottery machine. Not loudly. Just persistent, like it had wronged him personally. Someone leaned against the coffee counter, stirring powdered creamer into a cup that already smelled burnt. The smell of hot dogs had soaked into the walls sometime in the late nineties and never left.

I looked down at my hand.

The cut had closed a little. A thin line now. Dark at the edges. It didn't look dramatic enough to justify the trouble. That felt right.

Bandages were in aisle three. I knew that without reading the sign. Some knowledge doesn't come from memory so much as repetition—the kind you don't notice stacking up until your body starts moving before you do.

The boxes on the shelves were too clean. Corners sharp. Tape lines unbroken. They hadn't been cut open yet. That part would come later, when someone with a blade and a deadline took them apart in back. For now they stood there pretending to be finished things.

I picked up a small pack of bandages. Plastic. Smooth. It weighed almost nothing. Everything sealed. Everything confident.

I set it back down.
Then picked it up again.

The counter was whiter than it needed to be.
Not clean—sealed.

A smooth, laminated brightness that didn't invite touch so much as tolerate it.

I set the box down first.

Perfect edges. No give. The plastic window caught the light and threw it back.

Then the money.

Folded too many times. Soft in places where it shouldn't be. When I opened my hand, a bit of dirt came with it. A grain fell and slid, stopping near the barcode square like it had wandered into the wrong neighborhood.

I watched it sit there.

The bandage tugged as I leaned. The corner had lifted again. A faint, rusty smear showed through the pad, already drying. I didn't adjust it.

Nothing happened.

The screen glowed. Numbers waited.

The machine made a low, patient sound—not yet.

I kept my eyes on the counter. On the white surface. On the faint shadow my hand made as it hovered there. I could feel the heat in my palm, the stick of old glue, the tight pull where skin met tape.

Another grain dropped.

This one darker.

I wiped it with my thumb. It spread instead of lifting.

The air thickened, like the room had decided to hold its breath.

The drawer snapped open. Metal on metal.

A sharp, final sound.

I didn't look up.

The box slid toward me. It made a clean noise against the counter. The money was gone.

I picked the box up. My thumb pressed where the plastic was thinnest. It flexed, just a little. The dirt left a dull print that didn't wipe away on the first try.

I didn't try again.

The bell rang behind me—too quick, too cheerful—already welcoming whatever came next.

Outside, the light felt different. Less exact.

I stopped under the awning and put the box into my pocket without opening it. The corner of the bandage caught on the fabric and pulled. I let it.

The street took me back without comment.

The sidewalk sloped down toward the pumps. Concrete patched so many times it had forgotten what it was fixing.

A man sat near the edge of the lot, back against the ice machine, legs stretched out like he'd been dropped there and decided not to get up again. A blanket the color of old newspapers was wrapped around his shoulders. One shoe on. One shoe gone. The remaining lace was knotted into something that had once tried to be careful.

He wasn't looking at me. He was watching the door. Not hungry. Not angry. Just attentive—like the door might say something important if he didn't miss it.

I slowed without meaning to. The bandage tugged when my thumb bent. I flexed it once, felt the adhesive complain, then settle. I flexed it again. This time it held.

The man reached down and pinched a cigarette from the ground near his heel. It was short. Burned close to the filter. He turned it in his fingers, checking which end still remembered fire. Then he lit it with a lighter that clicked twice before agreeing.

He exhaled sideways. Smoke slid along the ice machine and vanished.

"You got a light?" he asked, still not looking at me.

I didn't smoke. Not anymore. I shook my head before he finished the sentence. He nodded like that answered something else too.

A car pulled in fast. Brakes squealed. A woman jumped out, phone to her ear, voice sharp with the kind of urgency that thinks it's rare. She didn't see either of us. Or maybe she did and had already decided what to do with the sight.

The man adjusted the blanket. The fabric made a dry, tired sound. He noticed my hand then—the clean bandage, the pressed edges.

"Cut?" he said.

"Yeah."

"Box?"

I smiled without showing it. "Something like that."

He nodded again. Approval, maybe. Or recognition. He flicked ash onto the concrete, missed the crack he was aiming for, didn't correct it.

For a moment we stood there together, not sharing anything that could be counted. The ice machine kicked, then settled into its heavy, indifferent churn. A flattened cardboard box leaned against the trash can, its tape split, corners crushed past repair.

"Those things never stick," he said, finally looking at the bandage. "You think they will. They don't."

"I know," I said.

He took another drag, slow. "Still better than nothing."

I didn't answer. There wasn't a good shape for one.

He looked at me then. Not asking. Not thanking.

I pressed the bandage back down, feeling the grit bite into the edge of the cut. The glue held, but the skin pulled with it.

Neither of us blinked.

The bus stop stood under a rectangle of yellow light, its glass walls humming faintly each time a truck passed. One of the panels was cracked. The lines spread outward from a single point and then stopped, held in place by the thin film beneath the surface. Nothing fell.

I stood near the bench but didn't sit. The metal looked colder than the night air. I shifted my weight once and let it settle again.

The bus came alongside the curb and slowed. It eased in and settled. The brakes released with a tired hiss.

The doors opened.

Warm air spilled out, thin and worn, carrying the muted smell of rubber and old fabric. I stepped forward. The floor was higher than the curb. I lifted my foot and felt the edge beneath my sole, the brief imbalance before my weight transferred.

I moved toward the middle, where the light was dimmer and the windows reflected more than they revealed.

The seat flexed and held.

The doors closed. The bus pulled away. Outside, the stop slid backward, the yellow light shrinking until it lost its shape.

The vibration of the engine climbed through the frame and settled in my knees.

My hand lay on my leg. The bandage had lifted at one edge, darkened where it had picked up dust. It moved with the sway of the bus, back and forth, in time with something larger than itself.

The box of bandages stayed in my pocket. I felt its weight when the bus turned.

I didn't reach for it.

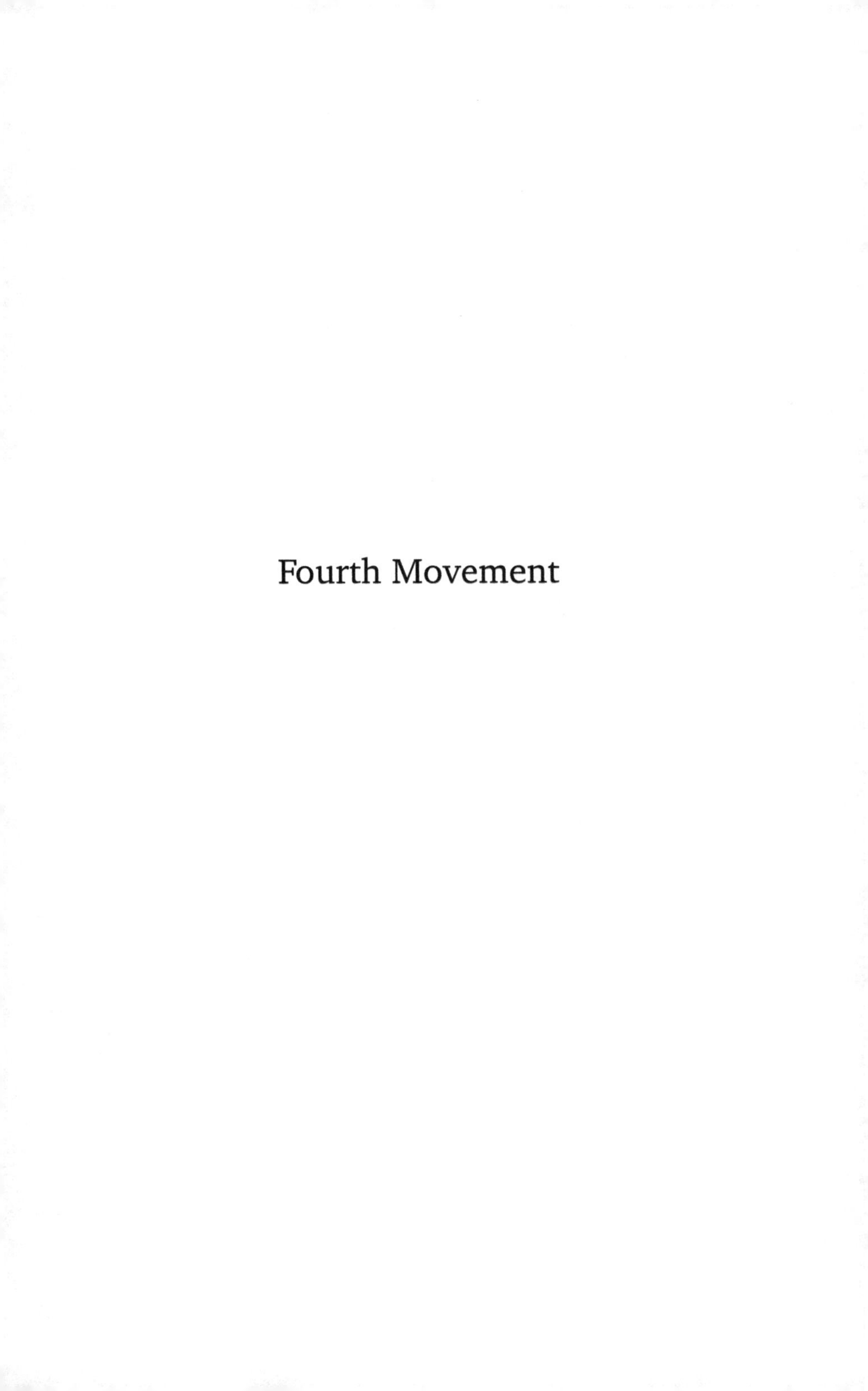

Fourth Movement

The glass was already broken when I noticed it.

Not shattered—just a clean crack running from the rim down toward the base, thin as a hair, sharp enough to catch light when the bus shifted.

The glass bottle was resting on the empty seat beside me.

Not upright.

Not placed carefully.

I didn't know how long it had been there.

It might have been forgotten.

It might have been set down once the crack appeared, no longer worth carrying.

The glass still held a little water.

No leak.

No drama.

I sat without touching it,
watching the line hold its place
as the bus leaned, then straightened.

There was nothing to fix.

Nothing to explain.

I knew—without thinking—that I would never use it.

Not because it was dangerous,
but because it no longer asked to be trusted.

Once a thing has changed,
it doesn't need to keep changing
to remain changed.

At my stop, I stood.
The glass stayed where it was.
No one reached for it.
    The bus smelled faintly of heat and fabric.
Not sweat—
just the warmed residue of coats
taken off and put back on
too many times to belong to anyone.
    I stood at first.
There was space to sit,
but it came and went
as people shifted.
    When I did sit,
it was near the back.
The vinyl was worn smooth,
creased where weight had learned to settle.
    At each stop,
the bus leaned,
then straightened.
    Across the aisle,
a man rested his elbow
on the metal rail.
His sleeve slid when the bus slowed,
caught again
when it picked up speed.
    He adjusted once.
Then stopped.
    The driver called out a stop I didn't need.
The doors opened.
Cold came in.
    When they closed,
the bus continued
as it had been.
    Nothing changed.
Nothing needed to.
    Two stops later,
the bus filled.

Someone stood close enough
that I could feel their weight
before they touched anything.
    A hand found the pole.
Another found the back of my seat.
    The seat shifted under it—
not much,
just enough
to register.
    I moved my knee an inch inward.
No one noticed.
    Outside, a delivery truck blocked half the lane.
The bus slowed,
then waited.
    I pressed my palm flat
against the seat beside me.
The vinyl was warm.
Softer than it looked.
    The bus lurched forward.
The hand on my seat tightened,
then lifted away.
    The seat kept its shape
for a moment longer than I expected.
Then it didn't.
    At my stop,
I stood carefully,
as if standing
could be done the wrong way.
    I stepped into the aisle
and moved toward the door.
    Behind me,
someone else sat down.
    The sidewalk was wet from an earlier melt.
Not slush—
just water darkening the concrete
in irregular patches
with no pattern to follow.

I walked along the edge of the block
where the curb dipped
slightly at the corner.
    A thin line of grit
had collected there.
    I stepped around it,
then stopped,
then stepped back
without knowing why.
    My shoe pressed into the wet concrete.
The sole held.
    Across the street,
a man shook out a cloth
before wiping a table
outside a closed café.
    He worked around a spot
that didn't come clean.
    When he finished,
the table looked the same
from where I stood.
    I waited for the light to change.
It took longer than I expected.
    Cars idled.
Someone coughed behind me.
    When the signal finally shifted,
no one moved right away.
    Then we did.
    The block was quiet on the far side of the street.
Not empty—
just spaced out
the way places get
between uses.
    A bicycle leaned against a fence
without a lock.
Its front wheel turned slightly
in the breeze,
then stopped.

I passed a storefront
with its lights on
and no one inside.
Shelves stocked.
Sign straight.
Hours posted on the glass
as if time
were still taking reservations.
My reflection moved with me
in the window.
It lagged by half a step,
just enough
to notice.
I slowed.
So did it.
At the corner,
a man waited for someone
who didn't arrive.
He checked his watch once,
then didn't again.
I stood there longer than necessary,
hands in my pockets,
feeling the coins shift
when I changed weight.
Nothing asked me
to decide.
The door beside me opened.
Warm air came out.
Then it closed.
I stayed where I was
until the light behind the glass
went off.
When I started walking again,
it wasn't toward anything in particular.
Just forward,
at a pace
that didn't require explanation.

A bus passed without stopping.
Not full.
Not empty.
Just not for me.
    Its windows slid by in a row,
faces briefly aligned,
then gone.
    I stood back from the curb,
farther than necessary,
close enough to feel
the wind it left behind.
    The schedule posted on the pole
had been peeled back once
and pressed down again.
    One corner lifted slightly
where the glue had thinned.
    I didn't smooth it.
    Across the street,
a man argued with a machine.
    He fed it a bill.
It took it.
Then did nothing.
    He waited.
Then pressed the same button again.
    The machine remained still.
    When it finally responded,
it did so without apology.
    Coins fell late,
clattering against one another
as if surprised
to be needed.
    The man gathered them carefully,
counting twice.
    I watched until he walked away.
    Another bus came.
This one slowed.
    I didn't raise my hand.

It stopped anyway.
The doors opened.
No one looked out.
I stepped forward,
then paused,
letting someone else go first.
They didn't hesitate.
When I followed,
the floor inside dipped slightly
under my weight.
Not enough
to matter.
I took a seat near the back.
Different bus.
Same vinyl.
This seat had no repair marks.
Just a faint crease
where the material had learned
how to fold.
I sat on the edge of it,
not fully committed.
Outside, the street moved on
without keeping time with me.
Inside, the bus pulled away.
No signal.
No agreement.
Just motion,
continuing.
The bench was colder than it looked.
Painted metal,
the kind that keeps its temperature
no matter how long it sits in the sun.
I lowered myself slowly,
testing the distance
before committing weight.
The bench didn't shift.
It never does.

When I leaned back,
something in my pocket
pressed forward
at an angle I hadn't planned for.
I adjusted once.
Then again,
smaller this time.
The pressure remained.
Not sharp.
Just present.
My hand hovered near my coat,
then dropped to my side.
Around me, the stop settled
into its usual pattern.
A woman checked her phone,
then put it away
without having learned anything.
A man paced the length of the curb,
counting steps
until the number stopped mattering.
The bus schedule rattled faintly
against its frame.
I shifted my weight to the other hip.
The pressure moved with me.
It wasn't asking.
It wasn't warning.
It was simply
where it was.
I stayed like that for a while,
breathing shallow enough
not to disturb anything.
When I stood again,
the bench kept its shape.
My coat didn't.
The pressure eased,
then settled back into place
as I began to walk.

I didn't check the pocket.
There was no need.
    The bus came full this time.
    People stood shoulder to shoulder,
hands already raised
before the doors opened.
    I stepped on last.
    There was nowhere to sit,
nowhere to lean
without borrowing something
already in use.
    I found a place near the rear door,
one hand on the rail,
the other resting
against my coat.
    The pressure in the pocket
shifted as the bus moved,
then settled again
when it stopped.
    No one reacted.
    A child cried once,
then stopped
when the sound failed
to draw attention.
    The bus lurched forward.
Bodies adjusted in sequence—
not together,
just fast enough
to avoid falling.
    I adjusted too.
    The pressure didn't change.
    At the next stop,
someone pushed past me
without looking.
    Their bag brushed my side.
The pocket pressed harder

for a moment,
then eased.
    Nothing followed.
    No look back.
No apology.
No recognition.
    The bus continued.
    I watched the doors
open and close
for stops that weren't mine.
    Each time,
air rushed in,
then was sealed out again.
    The pressure remained
unregistered.
    When my stop came,
I stepped off carefully,
making space where there wasn't much.
    The bus pulled away.
    On the sidewalk,
I stood still
until the movement inside me
caught up.
    People passed.
Traffic flowed.
A light changed somewhere overhead.
    The pocket was still there.
    So was everything else.

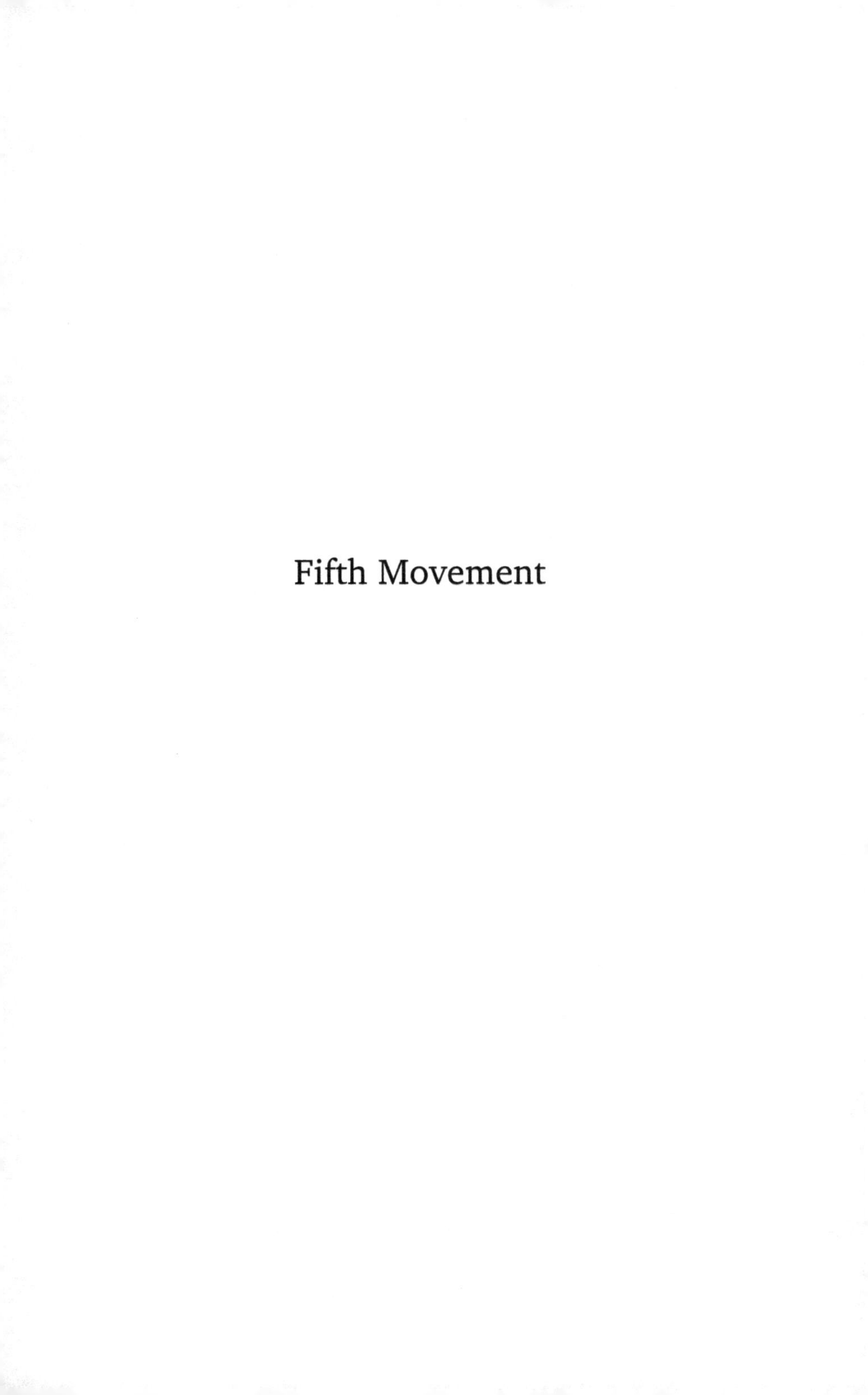

Fifth Movement

The bus stop emptied without ceremony.
     The advertisement box above the bench
stayed lit,
cycling through images
meant for people
who were no longer there.
     I stepped away from the curb
and followed the sidewalk
as it narrowed.
     My shoes sounded different here—
less echo,
more drag—
the pavement holding on
for half a second longer.
     Ahead, the park opened up
as a darker shape,
trees set back
from the path.
     The swings were still.
Their chains caught a bit of light
and gave it back
without moving.
     I walked along the edge,
where the grass met concrete,
keeping to the line
that required the least adjustment.

A dog passed with its owner,
a small green light
clipped to the collar,
rising and falling
with each step.
    We saw each other early.
There was time
not to react.
    The light moved on.
So did I.
    Halfway through the park,
my shoe struck something soft
and rolled.
    I stopped,
then bent down.
    A baseball,
scuffed along one seam,
familiar in the hand
before I thought about it.
    I carried it a few steps
and set it down
where it would be seen.
    The path curved west.
Streetlights grew closer together.
Houses came into focus
as shapes rather than addresses.
    My coat shifted as I walked.
The weight in the pocket
kept its place.
    I didn't slow down.
I didn't hurry.
    By the time the park fell behind me,
the street had already decided
how quiet it would be.

    The sidewalk narrowed again
where the park ended.

A turn to the west
cut the streetlight in half,
leaving the far side dimmer
than it needed to be.
    I walked there anyway.
    The buildings came in low pairs,
two floors,
windows stacked
without asking much of anyone.
    The path into the complex
was swept clean,
the concrete lighter
where it had been gone over twice.
    My steps slowed
without my telling them to.
    The keys shifted in my pocket.
The other weight didn't.
    I passed the gym wall,
its windows dark now,
the pool silent,
holding the day's noise
for later.
    Near the corner,
a light clicked on in a ground-floor unit
and stayed that way.
    I stopped at my door
and stood there longer
than was necessary
to open it.
    The handle was cool.
Familiar.
    When I turned the key,
the sound stayed close,
not echoing
the way it did outside.
    The door opened
just enough.

Inside, the air was still.
I stepped in
and closed it behind me,
careful not to let it latch
too hard.
    For a moment,
nothing moved.
    Then my coat settled,
the fabric folding
where it always did.
    The weight shifted
from walking
to standing.
    I stayed there,
not yet inside anything else.

    Inside, the room stayed dark.
Not unlit—
just unchanged.
    I left my shoes by the door,
toed them off
without bending.
    The floor was cooler
near the wall.
    I stepped there,
then back again,
learning where the temperature held.
    My coat came off
in one motion,
the sleeve catching briefly
at the wrist.
    I freed it
and hung the coat
where it always went.
    The fabric settled.
The pocket did not empty itself.

I moved the weight
from the coat
to the table by the door,
set down carefully,
as if sound still mattered.
    The table didn't react.
    I stood there,
hands open,
waiting for the room
to ask for something.
    It didn't.
    The refrigerator hummed once,
then stopped.
    I crossed the room
without turning on a light,
counting steps
that no longer needed counting.
    At the sink,
I rinsed my thumb
where the skin had split
near the nail.
    The cut was shallow.
It stung
only when water touched it.
    I dried it
and left it uncovered.
    The room held.
    I sat down
on the edge of the chair,
not using the back.
    Nothing shifted.
    For the first time that night,
I wasn't moving
and didn't feel
pulled to.
    The weight rested
where I had placed it.

The room did not close around me.
It simply stayed.

I lay down without setting an alarm.
The room kept its shape
when I did.
The ceiling fan was off.
Its blades held the air
as if they had forgotten
what motion was for.
I shifted once,
then stopped.
The mattress answered
by doing nothing new.
My thumb throbbed faintly,
not pain—
just a reminder
that the skin there
had given way earlier
and not been asked to explain.
I placed my hand
flat against the sheet
until the pulse faded
into something regular.
Outside, a car passed
and didn't return.
A pipe clicked
somewhere in the building,
then settled.
I counted my breaths
until the numbers lost interest
in being followed.
The weight was where I'd left it.
I knew this
without checking.
Sleep came close,
then pulled back,

the way animals do
when they don't trust the ground.
     I stayed still.
     Minutes gathered
without forming a line.
     At some point,
my thoughts loosened—
not into images,
not into stories—
just enough
to stop holding themselves together.
     I didn't go with them.
     I remained
where the room could find me
if it needed to.
     It didn't.
     Eventually,
the edge between waking and not
thinned.
     Not gone.
Just less certain.
     That was as far
as the night
was willing to go.

     I woke without opening my eyes.
Not fully—
just enough
to know the room
was still there.
     The air felt heavier
near the floor.
     I turned onto my side
and felt it change
along my ribs,
then settle again.

My thumb brushed the sheet.
The skin there caught slightly,
a dry pull
that made me stop.
     I adjusted the angle
instead of the hand.
     The clock on the stove
clicked once,
then held.
     I didn't check the time.
It wasn't asking.
     The weight stayed where it was.
I could feel its position
the way you feel
a chair behind you
without turning.
     Sleep approached again,
slower this time,
less interested
in being invited.
     My breathing deepened
on its own.
     Thoughts loosened further,
breaking into pieces
too small
to argue with one another.
     A sound formed—
not a word,
not an image—
then fell apart
before it reached me.
     I didn't follow it.
     The mattress warmed
where my shoulder pressed,
the heat spreading
only as far
as the pressure allowed.

    I stayed there,
neither moving forward
nor pulling back.
    Somewhere inside,
the need to stay alert
lost its footing.
    Not surrendered.
Just unbalanced.
    That was enough.

    A sound—
maybe from outside,
maybe from the building—
arrived without direction
and left the same way.
    I couldn't tell
if my eyes were open.
    There was no image
to check against.
    The sense of lying down
thinned,
as if the body had begun
to forget
what it was being supported by.
    I stayed where I was,
not because it felt right,
but because there was
no clearer alternative.
    Time passed
without lining itself up.
    Then even that
became a guess.
    For a moment—
not a moment measured,
just a slackening—
there was no forward
to lean into

and no back
to return to.
    Only this:
a place where direction
had stopped being useful.
    I did not move past it.
It moved past me.
    The sheet no longer marked
where I ended.
    My arm rested
somewhere against fabric,
but the pressure didn't return
a clear outline.
    I pressed my heel down,
then eased off,
watching how long it took
for the mattress
to remember me.
    It was slower than before.
    Breath moved through my chest
without rising much,
as if depth had become optional.
    I tried to swallow
and felt the motion
lose its destination halfway through.
    It completed itself anyway.
    The room remained present,
but not arranged.
    Objects kept their places
only by habit,
not by insistence.
    The table was still a table.
The door was still closed.
    That knowledge stayed intact,
floating,
no longer anchored
to position.

My thumb touched the pad
of my finger.
The split skin had sealed enough
to hold,
but not enough
to forget.
The sensation lingered
after contact ended,
a delay
without instruction.
I waited for the body to correct itself.
It didn't.
It adjusted.
Muscles softened
in places I hadn't asked them to,
while others stayed alert
without reason.
I stopped checking.
Somewhere beyond the walls,
a sound repeated—
not loud,
not regular—
and then ceased.
Nothing followed.
The sense of lying in a room
gave way
to something flatter,
less owned.
Not falling. Not floating.
Just no longer fully contained
by edges.
I stayed. The night did not advance.
It held.

Sixth Movement

I woke to the wrong sound.
    Not an alarm.
Not a voice.
    A wet, hollow thud,
followed by a scraping drag
along the concrete outside my door.
    I sat up too fast.
The room tilted,
then corrected itself
without asking.
    Another thud.
Closer.
    I stepped outside.
    The walkway lights were on,
evenly spaced,
doing what they always did.
    In the pool of light near the stairs,
a man lay on his side,
one arm folded under him
the wrong way.
    He was breathing.
That seemed important.
    A grocery bag had burst
near the bottom step.
    An orange had rolled clear
and come to rest
against the curb of the path.

So had a carton of eggs.
They had not survived.
   Yolk spread outward,
slow and bright,
finding the low places
in the concrete.
   I picked up the orange
and set it back
within the man's reach.
   It didn't change anything.
   From above,
a door opened.
Light spilled down the stairs.
   Someone said his name.
   I didn't look up.
   "They're here," I said.
   I stepped back
and closed my door.
   The latch caught harder
than I meant it to.
   Inside,
the room returned
without comment.
   The weight was still
where I had left it.
   I stood there for a moment,
listening as voices
rearranged themselves
outside.
   Nothing in me
asked to go back out.

   Inside, the room took a moment
to catch up.
   I stood by the sink
and turned the tap on.

Water ran over my thumb,
cool and steady.
The skin there pulled slightly
where it had split,
a thin reminder
that the grip earlier
had not gone unnoticed.
I rubbed my fingers together
once,
then again,
until the faint tack of citrus
gave way
to plain water.
I turned the tap off carefully,
listening for the moment
the pipe would answer back.
It didn't.
From outside came the sound
of feet on the stairs,
a door opening,
then voices—
not loud,
but layered,
moving past one another
without settling.
A phone rang somewhere above me.
Stopped.
The refrigerator clicked on,
worked against the noise,
then paused.
I dried my hand
and left the towel on the counter
where it landed.
The weight stayed on the table.
I didn't look at it.
I knew where it was
the way you know

where a wall is
when sound fails
to map the room.
    Outside, something scraped,
then lifted.
    A car door closed.
    The voices thinned,
but didn't disappear.
    I leaned my hip
against the counter
and let the pressure hold,
waiting for the room
to finish deciding
what it would keep.
    Eventually,
it did.
    The remaining sounds
fell back into their places,
smaller now,
no longer asking
to be sorted.
    I turned off the light
that I hadn't meant to turn on.
    The room returned
to its reduced shape.
    I lay back down
without adjusting anything.
    The mattress received me
the same way it had before.
    Whatever had happened
outside
did not follow me in.
    Not completely.

    My thumb began to ache
after I'd stopped
paying attention to it.

    Not sharply.
Just enough
to pull the hand forward
on its own.
    I flexed the joint once
and felt the skin resist,
then give
without tearing.
    The sensation stayed
a fraction longer
than the motion that caused it,
as if the body
had filed it
somewhere else.
    I lay still
and waited
for the ache
to turn into something useful.
    It didn't.
    Instead,
my shoulder tightened,
then released,
without asking permission.
    A calf muscle twitched.
Stopped.
    Breath shifted
to a shallower register
and stayed there.
    Nothing connected.
    The room remained quiet,
but not blank.
    Small sounds—
the building settling,
a distant car—
arrived late,
as if routed through
the wrong path.

I turned my head
and felt a brief lag
before the pillow answered back.
    It caught up.
Too quickly.
    My fingertips still felt
slightly wrong—
dry,
faintly slick—
as if something had been there
and wasn't now.
    I pressed my thumb
against the mattress
until the ache
flattened into heat,
then let go.
    The heat stayed.
    Somewhere in the body,
a sequence had been interrupted
and resumed
out of order.
    There was no correction.
    I stopped looking for one.
    The night held,
unevenly.

    The ache spread
without choosing a direction.
    It didn't travel.
It appeared.
    Behind the knee,
a dull pressure surfaced,
then receded
before I could place it.
    My jaw tightened briefly,
as if bracing

for a sound
that never came.
    I opened my mouth
and closed it again.
The muscles complied late.
    Breath caught once
at the top of an inhale,
held longer than needed,
then released
with a soft collapse.
    The body seemed to check itself
and find things
out of sequence.
    I lay flat
and let it happen.
    A memory tried
to attach itself
to the sensation—
failed—
and slid away.
    No images followed.
    The pressure in my thumb
returned,
lighter now,
but wider,
as if the original point
had lost authority.
    I shifted my weight
by a few inches
and felt the mattress
answer in stages.
    The delay remained.
    Outside,
a sound rose
and cut off.
    Inside,
nothing adjusted to meet it.

The room kept its reduced shape,
but the body
no longer fit it exactly.
    Edges softened.
Not gone—
just unreliable.
    I stayed still,
because movement
no longer promised relief.
    Eventually,
the sensations thinned,
not resolving,
just losing coherence.
    They left behind
a vague map
that didn't match the territory.
    I did not redraw it.
    The night remained unfinished.

    My body prepared
for a movement
I did not make.
    The impulse arrived first—
a tightening in the thigh,
a shift in balance—
then waited.
    Nothing followed.
    A moment later,
the impulse withdrew,
leaving behind
a faint tremor,
as if it had misjudged
the timing.
    Breath shortened,
anticipating effort.
    There was none.

The chest held the shape
a little too long,
then corrected itself.
    I lay still
and felt these small rehearsals
start and stop,
each one convinced
it knew what usually came next.
    None of them did.
    My hand twitched,
expecting resistance.
    The sheet did not answer
where it thought it would.
    The thumb pressed down,
then released,
testing for pain
that had already moved on.
    Heat lingered
without purpose.
    Somewhere deeper,
muscle and nerve
ran through a sequence
that used to end cleanly.
    Now it dissolved
before reaching its mark.
    The body paused,
as if waiting
for what usually followed.
    Nothing arrived.
    A slow fatigue spread—
not tiredness,
but the cost
of being wrong repeatedly.
    I adjusted my position
by less than an inch
and felt relief

that lasted
no longer than the motion.
    After that,
even anticipation
began to thin.
    The body stopped guessing.
    It held itself
in a neutral state,
ready
but unconvinced.
    Nothing resolved.
Nothing escalated.
    The night continued
without offering
a next step.

    Time did not stretch.
It misplaced itself.
    A breath completed
and felt as if it belonged
to an earlier moment,
arriving late.
    Another followed
too soon,
crowding the space
it expected to have.
    I tried to count
and found the numbers
arriving out of order.
    Two came before one.
Then nothing.
    The body noticed
before I did.
    Muscles released
on a cue
that had already passed.

The release still happened.
It landed
without context.
I shifted my head
and felt the pillow respond
as if it had been waiting
for a slightly different angle.
The response was correct.
The timing wasn't.
A sound from outside—
brief, indistinct—
registered
after it was gone.
I knew it had happened
without knowing when.
Inside,
the sense of sequence
thinned further.
Actions still led to effects,
but not beside them.
The thumb pulsed once,
then again,
the second beat arriving
before the first had finished.
They overlapped,
cancelled,
left nothing to count.
I lay there
without assembling
what should come next.
Expectation lost its anchor.
Moments gathered
without lining up,
each one complete,
none following.
The body adjusted
by doing less—

holding fewer positions,
releasing sooner.
   This did not restore order.
It reduced the damage.
   Eventually,
even the idea of "next"
fell out of use.
   The night continued
as a set of arrivals
without sequence.
   I remained there,
present
in whatever order
the body accepted.

   The floor stayed below me.
   I confirmed it
by shifting my heel
until the pressure returned
where it always did.
   Light leaked in from the edge of the curtain,
a narrow band
that did not move
when I did.
   I sat up slowly and felt gravity
complete its work.
   The room arranged itself
around fixed points:
the table by the door,
the chair,
the line where wall met floor.
   I placed my feet down
one at a time
and waited
for the delay to finish.
   It did.

Breath settled
into a rhythm
that belonged to the body,
not to my thoughts.
The thumb still ached,
but the ache had a place.
It stayed there.
I stood.
The floor held.
I took a step.
Then another.
Outside, a car passed.
It did not return.
I reached for the table
and touched its edge,
wood unmoving.
Things stayed
where they were
after I let go.
I stood there
a moment longer,
not resting,
just confirming
that the order held
without my attention.
It did.
I turned toward the sink,
already knowing
where it would be.
The day had not begun.
But the world
was ready for it
whenever it did.

Seventh Movement

The room was clear.
    Not brighter—
exact.
    Edges held
without effort.
The table kept its corners.
The chair did not soften
when attention drifted.
    Everything present
had already arrived.
    On the tabletop,
objects occupied
the same surface
without touching.
    The box was there,
closed,
its weight unchanged.
    Nearby,
a thin skin of yellow
had dried flat
against the wood.
    An orange rested
near the edge,
unbroken,
its color intact.
    None of these
asserted sequence.

Light crossed the room
from more than one direction.
    A cool band cut low.
Another fell straight down,
hard enough
to fix a shadow.
A third lingered by the wall,
amber,
without warmth.
    The shadows disagreed.
They extended
in different directions
from the same object
and did not correct.
    I was seated.
    This was registered
through pressure—
the chair holding,
the floor below.
    Nothing drifted.
    Sound entered
without bringing a source.
    Water moved somewhere,
steady,
drawn inward.
    A dull impact followed,
once,
without a body to complete it.
    Then an engine turned,
caught,
and stopped.
    The sounds shared the space
without overlap.
    My hands rested
where they had been placed.

Muscle tension
completed itself
and remained.
The room did not advance.
It did not withdraw.
All realized moments
occupied the same plane—
not stacked,
not aligned—
simply present.
Nothing asked to be chosen.
A position was being held.

One hand was raised.
The motion had already finished
by the time it registered.
The arm occupied
a new relation
to the table.
Fingers closed
around nothing.
Not air.
Not space.
Nothing
entered the grasp.
Light passed between
skin and surface
without bending.
No resistance
was available.
The arm lowered.
The chair received
the shift.
The floor took the weight.
The box remained closed
without reference
to distance.

The orange did not roll.
The dried skin did not crack.
    A slight lean forward
had occurred.
    Shadows adjusted
without agreeing
on direction.
    Sound continued
without alignment.
    Water drew itself inward.
An engine turned once
and left no heat.
    Another impact arrived—
duller—
and settled
without a corresponding action.
    Contact occurred
at the edge of the table.
    It ended.
    Nothing followed.
    Pressure was recorded
without extension.
    The palm rested flat.
    The surface held.
    What had happened
remained what it was.
    What had not
did not present itself
for repetition.
    Limits were in place.
    They did not announce themselves.

    The angle
of my head
had changed.
    For a moment,
there was no corresponding awareness—

only the new arrangement
holding its place.
    The movement had already arrived
at its coordinate.
    It did not require a beginning.
It offered no follow-up.
    Perception caught up
without completing a loop.
    The chair continued
to support what it was given.
The floor remained below.
    Across the table,
nothing rearranged itself
in response.
    Light crossed the surface
from incompatible directions.
    The shadows kept their disagreement.
    Sound entered and ended
without asking
to be located.
    A position was being occupied.
    Not chosen.
Not confirmed.
    The room stayed exact.
    So did the constraint
that allowed it.

    A shift was registered
before any intention formed.
    The position being occupied
no longer matched
the one that had been held.
    This was not announced.
    The chair remained where it was.
The table kept its edge.
    Light did not alter its angles
to acknowledge the change.

Only the relation
between surfaces
had updated.
    Weight redistributed itself
without requesting balance.
    The body accepted
the new arrangement
as if it had always been there.
    Across the table,
the objects did not react.
    The box stayed closed.
The orange held its distance.
The thin skin on the wood
did not lift.
    No sequence emerged
to explain the shift.
    Sound arrived again—
water,
then nothing—
and left no residue.
    A faint pressure
appeared along the spine,
not as pain,
but as alignment.
    It did not intensify.
It did not recede.
    The space around me
continued to present itself
without hierarchy.
    Foreground and background
refused to separate.
    Everything remained
equally available,
equally irrelevant.
    Another adjustment
had already completed
by the time it was noticed.

Awareness lagged,
then stopped trying
to synchronize.
What remained
was the state itself—
stable enough
to hold,
insufficient
to explain.
The room did not correct
the mismatch.
It allowed it.

Density increased
without accumulation.
Nothing new entered.
What was already there
pressed closer
without moving.
The table did not gain weight.
The air did not thicken.
Yet the interval
between things
narrowed.
Objects held their places
more firmly
than before.
The box remained closed,
but the space around it
tightened.
The orange did not approach.
Its distance
became exact.
Light intersected itself
and stopped.
Shadows overlapped
without blending.

No single edge
claimed priority.
    Sound failed to separate
into foreground.
    Water, impact, engine—
not layered,
not sequential—
compressed
into a single register
that refused depth.
    The body registered
the increase
not as pressure,
but as cost.
    Breath shortened
without distress.
    Muscle tone adjusted
to conserve
what did not need
to be spent.
    Another shift
completed itself
and left no trace
of passage.
    Awareness arrived late,
took note,
and withdrew.
    Nothing required response.
    The density did not ask
to be resolved.
    It did not advance.
    It simply remained
too present
to ignore,
too stable
to oppose.

Something did not carry through.
There was no break.
No collapse.
One relation simply
failed to remain
alongside the others.
The table stayed.
The chair stayed.
Light continued
to cross the surface
from incompatible directions.
But the exact distance
between two objects
no longer held.
Not reduced.
Not increased.
Unmaintained.
The body adjusted
before awareness arrived.
Muscle tone released
what it had been holding
without instruction.
Breath shortened again,
this time
without correction.
A faint warmth
appeared
along the forearms—
not spreading,
not intensifying—
as if effort
had already been spent
and could not be recovered.
The box remained closed.
The orange remained whole.

But they no longer pressed
equally
on the space between them.
    One relation had been dropped.
    No record marked
which one.
    Sound thinned.
    Water receded
into a narrower channel.
    The engine's presence
lost its edge.
    Only one register
remained clear.
    The body followed it
without choosing.
    Another configuration
had already taken hold
by the time it was noticed.
    This one required
less.
    The density eased,
not by removal,
but by subtraction
of obligation.
    What remained
fit.
    Not because it was correct,
but because it could continue
without generating excess.
    The room stayed exact.
    Fewer relations
were being maintained
within it.

    Clarity remained
where alignment still held.

Elsewhere,
nothing failed—
there was simply
less to connect.
    Edges stayed sharp
until they no longer mattered.
    The table kept its outline.
The chair kept its weight.
    But the space between them
no longer supported
a continuous account.
    Attention crossed it
and found no purchase.
    Light continued
to arrive intact.
    It did not blur.
    It landed
and stopped short
of linking surfaces
that no longer shared
a maintained relation.
    Shadows ended abruptly,
as if cut
by an absence
that cast none of its own.
    Depth did not collapse.
It hollowed.
    The body registered this
as ease.
    Less adjustment
was required.
    Muscle tone settled
into a narrower band.
    The faint warmth
along the arms
did not spread.

It dissipated
by no longer being fed.
    Across the table,
the box remained.
So did the orange.
    But the line
that once accounted
for both
no longer persisted.
    One could be present
without the other
needing to remain legible.
    Sound reached the room
and stopped
at uneven boundaries.
    Some frequencies
found no continuation.
    They ended
without decay.
    A region of the room
no longer participated
in sequence.
    It did not darken.
    It simply
was not addressed.
    The room stayed exact.
    Not everywhere.
    Only where relations
were still being held.

    Exactness persisted
without covering the whole.
    Where it held,
objects retained
their edges.
    Where it did not,
no error appeared—

only a loosening
of obligation.
    Across the table,
the box and the orange
no longer defined
a boundary between them.
    Not nearer.
Not farther.
    The distance ceased
to require distinction.
    Neither displaced the other.
Neither demanded precedence.
    Their earlier exclusion
did not reverse.
    It thinned.
    Light reached both
without needing to decide
which it served.
    Shadows overlapped
and stopped caring
about agreement.
    The surface beneath them
did not reconcile the view.
    It did not need to.
    A relation that once insisted
on separation
failed to renew itself.
    Nothing replaced it.
    The space between
no longer enforced
either/or.
    It accepted
both without integration.
    The body registered
a reduction in effort.
    No correction was prepared.

The hands remained
where they had been placed.
    No reach assembled itself.
    Sound arrived again—
not louder,
not clearer—
simply present
where sequence
no longer applied.
    A region of the room
continued to participate.
Another did not.
    Neither claimed authority.
    What remained exact
did not expand.
    What fell out
did not return.
    The room persisted
as a set of held relations
surrounded by areas
no longer asked
to be maintained.
    Within that condition,
nothing needed to be chosen.
    Not because choice was denied,
but because the structure
no longer required it.

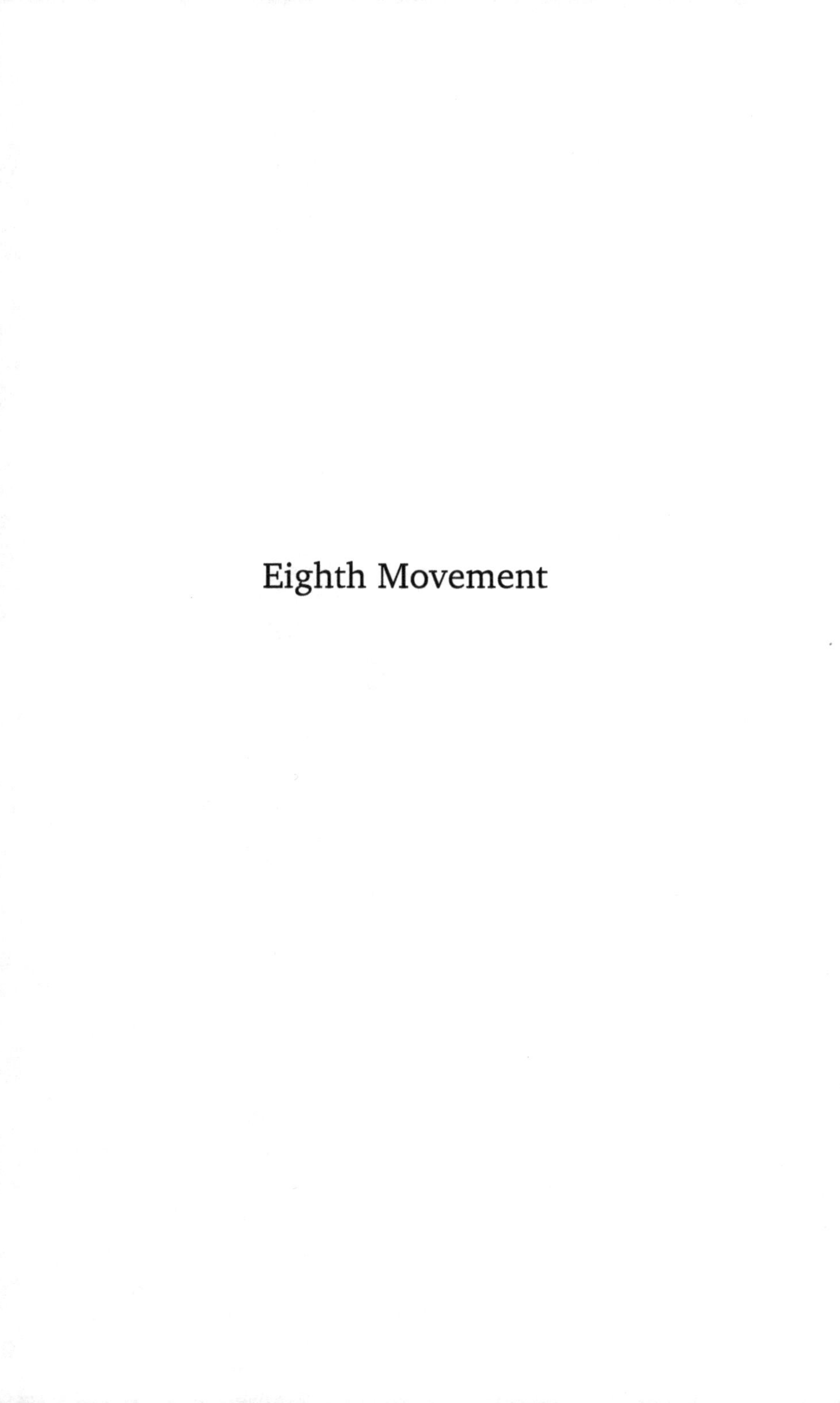

Eighth Movement

It was morning.
    Light was already in the room.
It reached the wall
before anything else did.
    The curtain held part of it.
The rest passed through.
The air was cool.
Not cold.
    The floor kept the night
without comment.
Walls remained
at their distances.
    The table stood.
The chair stood.
    Nothing had been arranged
for this hour,
yet nothing was out of place.
    The box was where it had been.
Closed.
No reason appeared
to open it.
    Outside, sound occurred.
    A car passed.
A door closed somewhere else.
Footsteps crossed
and did not return.

They did not wait
to be noticed.
    Inside, the body was upright.
Weight settled
where weight settles.
    There was no correction.
    Breath moved
at a pace
that did not need supervision.
    The hands stayed
where they were.
    No task gathered around them.
    Nothing suggested
that something had ended.
Nothing suggested
that something was beginning.
    The day was already
in use.
    This room
had not been excluded
from it.
    That condition
did not ask
to be named.
    It was enough
to continue
being here.

    The light shifted
without becoming brighter.
It moved along the wall
as the room continued
to be used.
    The sink held a small sound
when the tap was turned.
Water came
and stopped.

No adjustment followed.
The counter was clear
enough
to remain so.
Nothing waited there.
The body leaned
for a moment
and straightened again.
That was all.
Outside, another car passed.
It did not slow.
Air entered
when a window was opened
a few inches.
It carried no message.
The temperature changed
slightly.
Enough to notice.
Not enough to respond.
The floor accepted weight
where it was placed.
The shoes stayed on.
There was no reason
to remove them yet.
Time did not announce itself.
It proceeded
by continuing.
What had been present
remained present.
What had not
did not arrive.
This did not require
attention.
It only required
that nothing interfere.
The room allowed that.
So did the day.

The light reached the edge
of the table
and stopped.
    It did not insist
on going farther.
    Dust showed briefly
and then did not.
    The surface remained usable.
    The body shifted weight
from one foot
to the other.
    The change completed
before it was noticed.
    Balance did not ask
to be checked.
    The hands moved once—
not toward anything,
not away.
    They returned
to where they had been.
    Outside, a voice crossed
the space between buildings.
    It was not meant
for this room.
    It passed.
    The air settled again.
Nothing followed it in.
    The room kept
its proportions.
    Distance stayed reliable.
    The day continued
without narrowing its options.
    There was no signal
to hurry.
There was no signal
to stop.

What mattered
was not identified.
What did not matter
was not listed.
The body remained
available.
That condition
did not change.
It did not need
to be held.

The light stayed
where it had reached.
It did not move back.
The room required
a second look
to confirm
that nothing had shifted.
The confirmation
took longer
than before.
The body adjusted
its stance
and held it
for an extra moment.
Balance settled,
but not immediately.
The floor felt
slightly firmer
than it had earlier.
Not different.
Just more present.
The hands paused
before resting again.
No task had formed.
Still, the pause remained.

Outside, a sound repeated—
the same distance,
the same direction.
    It did not register
as new.
    It registered
as still happening.
    Air moved through the room
and stopped.
    The temperature held.
    The body noticed
the holding.
    Breath continued,
but attention
did not fully leave it.
    Nothing asked
to be done.
Nothing failed.
    Yet the effort
to remain unengaged
was no longer free.
    The room stayed usable.
So did the day.
    They required
a little more care
to keep that way.

    Attention did not spread
as easily as before.
    It gathered
and stayed closer
to the body.
    The light held
its position.
    The edges it touched
remained clear.

Others required
a moment longer
to resolve.
The body shifted again.
This time,
the movement finished
with a slight correction.
Not visible.
Just enough
to be felt.
The hands rested
and stayed there.
They did not wander.
Sound entered
and left
without layering.
Each instance
stood alone.
None carried over.
The air felt still,
then less so.
The change was small.
It asked
to be noticed.
Breath continued
at the same pace,
but its rhythm
no longer disappeared
on its own.
It needed
to be allowed.
Nothing demanded action.
Nothing promised ease.
The room remained usable.
The day remained open.
Maintaining that
now required

attention
to remain intact.
    Not more.
Just present.

    A sound arrived
from farther away
than the room.
    Not louder.
Just less contained.
    It crossed
without seeking entry.
    The window held.
    The air shifted
in response,
then settled again.
    The body noticed
the change
and did not follow it.
    Weight stayed
where it had been placed.
    The floor remained reliable,
though attention
checked it once more
than necessary.
    Outside, movement continued
without reference
to this space.
    It did not pause.
    Inside, the room
kept its order.
    Not arranged.
Just intact.
    The light no longer felt new.
    It was simply there,
doing its work.

    The body adjusted
its position
by a small degree
and stopped.
    That was enough.
    Nothing pressed inward.
Nothing withdrew.
    The boundary
between here and elsewhere
held
without needing reinforcement.
    Continuing
now required
awareness of that boundary.
    Not vigilance.
Just care.

    The body moved
before the movement
was required.
    Not away.
Not toward.
    Just enough
to clear space
that had not yet
become a problem.
    The chair shifted
a few inches.
    It did not scrape.
    The sound it made
stopped
before becoming noticeable.
    That mattered.
    The room accepted
the adjustment
without change.

    Light continued
to fall
where it had been falling.
    Outside, a door closed.
    It closed
for reasons
unrelated to this place.
    The boundary held.
    Attention remained
narrow.
    Not tense.
Focused.
    The hands did not lift.
    They stayed available.
    Nothing asked
to be prevented.
Nothing needed
to be corrected.
    The cost
of remaining
was small,
but no longer invisible.
    It was paid
without comment.
    The day continued
to move past the room.
    The room continued
to be used.
    Neither required
acknowledgment.
    Care
did not announce itself.
    It simply
reduced friction
enough
for everything else
to keep going.

The light remained.
It did not deepen.
It did not withdraw.
The room held
its current arrangement.
Nothing in it
requested revision.
The body stood
where it stood.
No adjustment followed.
Weight remained distributed.
Balance remained sufficient.
Breath continued
without needing
to be noticed.
Attention narrowed
to what was necessary
and no farther.
Outside, movement persisted.
It did not intersect
with this space.
The boundary did not fail.
It did not soften.
It held.
The day proceeded
without reference.
This room
was not consulted.
What could continue
did.
What could not
did not.
The system settled
into its present condition.
Stable.
Limited.
Operational.

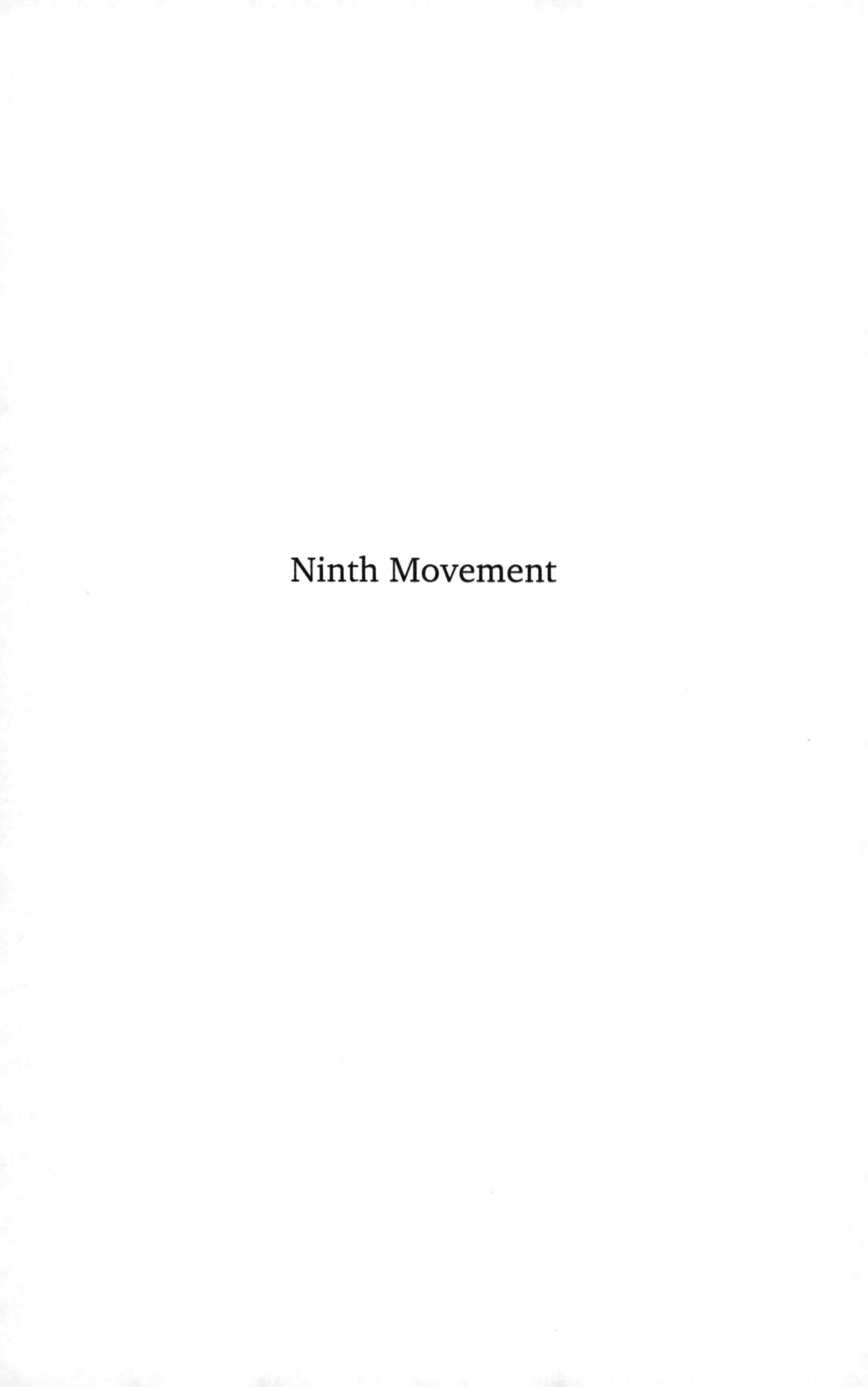

Ninth Movement

A sound entered the room
that did not belong to the day's background.
Small. Uneven.
    The room did not reject it.
It adjusted.
    Footsteps crossed the floor quickly—
weight heavier than the ones that followed.
A door opened.
The light did not change.
    "Washing your face?" his son said,
glancing at the sink.
"You just get up?"
    "In a minute."
    "You sleep late!"
    She came in.
Red jacket.
One pigtail sat higher than the other.
    He smiled.
"A little."
    She tipped her head back,
as if looking through the ceiling.
    "Is your dad's star the brightest one?" she asked.
    "Yes," he said,
only his mouth visible behind the towel.
    Her father reached out,
trying to fix the lower pigtail.
She turned her head away.

"Grandpa, did you see Lolli?" she asked.
"I forgot it last time."
    "It's on the shelf by the TV."
    She ran toward the living room.
    "One of the cooks cut his hand," his son said.
"I have to cover.
Can you keep her?"
    "Of course," he said.
"You go ahead."
    His son's eyes caught the box of bandages.
He picked it up without opening it.
    "I'll take this."
    The door closed.
The sound of the car did not linger.
    "Found it."
    She came back holding the felt rabbit—
one ear bent where it never stayed straight.
She pressed it once to her chest,
then checked the ear,
then checked it again.
    The room returned to its earlier proportions,
but not to its earlier state.
Something had been added
that did not leave a mark.

    They walked.
Red jacket.
Dark blue coat.
    The swings were moving,
pushed by adults
who did not look up.
    Farther out,
the field was empty.
No lines. No practice.
Only green,
open, unclaimed.

The place
where the baseballs
had been set
was bare.
    He noticed.
    She ran ahead,
stopped,
then ran again.
    He followed
at a pace
that did not try
to match hers.
    The grass bent and returned.
    Shoes left faint impressions
that did not hold.
    Nearby, a parent called a name.
The name answered.
Neither belonged to them.
    The sky was full of cloud—
not heavy, not dramatic,
just moving.

    Inside, the room was.
    A pot was on the stove.
Tiny bubbles had already begun
to map the bottom of the steel.
    She circled the stove once,
then again,
watching the blue flame
as if it were something
that could be hurried by looking.
    "Is it boiling?" she asked.
    "Almost."
    "Now?" she said, leaning in.
    "Now," he said,
and dropped the pasta in—

short, curved tubes
that settled quickly.
    "How long?"
    "Four minutes," he said.
"That's all."
    She watched the pot
as the water changed its sound,
waiting for the transition.
    In another pot,
the chicken was already done.
He took a piece,
blew on it steadily
until the heat let go,
and held it out.
    She opened her mouth without ceremony.
Took it.
Chewed slowly,
serious about it.
    "Hot," she said,
but she did not stop.
    "It's supposed to be," he said.
    She watched him turn the heat down.
    "Is it ready?"
    "In a minute."
    "Now?"
    "Now," he said.
    He drained the pasta
as it reached its shape.
Poured the broth from the second pot.
Clear.
Simple.
    Steam rose
and thinned.
    She sat across from him
and used a fork.
The tines clicked against the bowl—
once, then again—

not loud,
just there.
    "My dad's noodles aren't as good as yours," she said.
    He did not answer right away.
    "Why don't you teach him?" she asked.
    "He has his own way," he said.
    She accepted that
and kept eating.
    When the bowl was empty,
she leaned back
and looked at her rabbit.
She pressed the bent ear flat,
let it spring back.

    The dishes stayed on the table.
    Outside, a car waited.
    His son was in the driver's seat,
leaning down
so he could be seen through the window.
He waved once.
    She climbed right up to the back window.
Pressed her face to the glass,
holding Lolli up
so it waved too—
the bent ear shaking with the motion.
    He stood on the sidewalk
and watched the car
until it turned the corner.
    The space where it had been remained.
    This place
was sufficient
to keep.

    He went back inside.
He turned off the light.
    In the dark,
the room did not disappear.

It held.

Outside,
the world
went on.

To the Reader

This book does not offer healing.
It does not promise meaning.
It does not mediate what it presents.

What follows is a record of a prolonged and precise failure of
understanding.
This failure does not arise from neglect or lack of effort.
It emerges when an observer applies the most rigorous tools
available—
physical reasoning, structural attention, and sustained logical
consistency—
to forms of damage that do not admit repair.

Across these chapters, you will encounter a system attempting
to maintain order
after the loss of a central narrative.

If what follows feels distant or offers little consolation,
it is because these movements do not attempt to shield the
observer
from the conditions they describe.
They remain where the world has placed them,
and do not seek to be otherwise.